GROWING GARDENS

Vegetable Gardens

BY MATT LILLEY

Kids Core
An Imprint of Abdo Publishing
abdobooks.com

abdobooks.com

Cover Photo: Viktor Sergeevich/Shutterstock Images
Interior Photos: SDI Productions/E+/Getty Images, 4–5; Plan Shooting2/Imazins/Getty Images, 7; Shutterstock Images, 8, 10–11, 21, 26, 28 (top), 28 (bottom), 29 (top), 29 (bottom); Vera Prokhorova/Shutterstock Images, 13; Denis Pogostin/Shutterstock Images, 14, 18; Westend61/Getty Images, 16–17; Bell Ka Pang/Shutterstock Images, 22; Eduard Goricev/Shutterstock Images, 25

Editor: Christa Kelly
Series Designer: Katharine Hale

Library of Congress Control Number: 2024948987

Publisher's Cataloging-in-Publication Data

Names: Lilley, Matt, author.
Title: Vegetable gardens / by Matt Lilley
Description: Minneapolis, Minnesota: Abdo Publishing, 2026 | Series: Growing gardens | Includes online resources and index.
Identifiers: ISBN 9781098297435 (lib. bdg.) | ISBN 9798384919957 (ebook)
Subjects: LCSH: Gardens--Juvenile literature. | Gardening--Juvenile literature. | Vegetables--Juvenile literature. | Horticulture--Juvenile literature.
Classification: DDC 635.1--dc23

CONTENTS

People in cooler climates can start planting outdoors as soon as the ground warms.

CHAPTER 1

Growing Fresh Food

It was a spring day. Tia was in her garden. She scooped up a handful of soil. It was warm and dry. This meant it was time to plant her first vegetables.

Tia started digging. She broke up dirt clumps. She pulled up dead plants and weeds.

Next, Tia pressed holes into the dirt. She put a few spinach seeds in each hole. She planted lettuce a few feet away. Finally, she covered the seeds with dirt and watered the garden patch.

Tia picked up her tools. It was still too cold to plant other vegetables. She would have to plant cucumbers and eggplants another day.

Tomatoes

Many people grow tomatoes. There are thousands of kinds of tomatoes. Different types of tomatoes have different flavors. Each type may also have different needs. Some tomatoes need a lot of space. Others are small. Different types of tomatoes may also take different amounts of time to grow.

By summer, Tia would have plenty of fresh vegetables!

Vegetable Gardens

Gardeners grow many types of food. Vegetables are especially popular. Many people use the word *vegetable* as a cooking term. It refers to **edible** plants that are not sweet. Cauliflower and green beans are vegetables.

Vegetables are grouped into categories based on which part of the plant gets eaten. There are three main types. Underground vegetables are foods grown for their roots, **tubers**, and **bulbs**. Carrots and potatoes are underground vegetables. Aboveground vegetables are foods grown for their leaves, stems, and flowers. Broccoli is grown for its flowers. Spinach is grown for its leaves. This makes these plants aboveground vegetables. Fruit vegetables are grown for their fruits and seeds. Tomatoes and cucumbers are fruit vegetables.

Vegetable gardening is a fun and rewarding activity. It helps people connect with nature. It also allows gardeners to grow delicious food.

Explore Online

Look at the website below. Does it give any new information about growing vegetables that wasn't in Chapter One?

Grow Your Own Garden

abdocorelibrary.com/vegetable -gardens

Community gardens are
shared spaces where people
can garden.

CHAPTER 2

Planning a Vegetable Garden

When planning a garden, people should first decide where to grow their plants. There are many options. Some people have big gardens in yards. Others have small gardens on porches. Still others have spaces in community gardens.

When choosing a garden spot, people should find an area that gets lots of sunlight. Most vegetables need lots of sun. It gives them the energy to grow.

Choosing Plants

Next, gardeners should choose which plants to grow. Gardeners should pick vegetables they want to eat. They should also choose vegetables that will grow well in their gardens.

Loamy Soil

Vegetables grow best in loamy soil. This is soil that contains 40 percent sand, 40 percent silt, and 20 percent clay. Loamy soil allows roots to breathe. It also allows plants to get just enough water.

Space is one factor gardeners should consider. A small porch garden will not have space for plants that take up a lot of room.

Broccoli grows best in cooler temperatures.

Climate is another factor that gardeners should consider. Some vegetables grow best in hot climates. Other plants grow best in cooler areas.

Laura Fernandez is a chef and gardener. She tells beginner gardeners:

> Don't be afraid to fail! We can learn so much from our failures. Gardening is a practice in patience and has become my greatest teacher. Start small and **gradually** add each year.

Source: Tiffany Deluccia. "Interview: Front-Yard Vegetable Gardening." *GVL Gardening,* 17 July 2022, newsletter.gvlgardening.com. Accessed 24 Sept. 2024.

Point of View

What is the author's point of view on this topic? What is your point of view? Write a short essay about how they are similar or different.

People can buy seeds, plant containers, soil, and garden tools at garden stores.

Growing Vegetables

Once people have chosen their plants, it is time to start gardening! Most people begin planting outside in the spring. But many vegetables can be started earlier indoors. Gardeners can plant the seeds in containers. This gives them more time to grow.

Pepper plants need six to eight hours of sunlight each day.

Once the ground warms, people can get ready to put their plants in the ground. Gardeners can start by preparing their gardens' soil. They should break up any dirt clumps. They should also pull any weeds or unwanted plants out of the garden beds. Some people add fertilizer or compost. These mixtures give the soil extra **nutrients**.

When to Plant

Different vegetables should be planted at different times. Leafy greens can be planted early in the spring. They do well in cool weather. Root vegetables can be planted early too. They need lots of time to grow.

As the weather warms, more vegetables can be planted. Gardeners can plant squash, green beans, and tomatoes. Peppers and eggplants do best in hot weather. These should be planted last. They need plenty of sun.

Planting Vegetables

When planting vegetables, it is important to leave space between each plant. This gives each plant enough room to grow. Gardeners planting seeds should read the instructions on the seed packets. These packets usually say how far apart each plant should be. The packets will also say how deep the seeds should be planted.

Gardeners planting seeds should poke a hole into the soil. Then they should put several seeds in each hole. This makes it more likely that at least one of the seeds will sprout.

When the plants are a few inches high, gardeners can pull seedlings that are too close to each other. This will give the others more space. People should write down when

What's on the Backs of Seed Packets?

When to plant

Planting instructions

How much sun a plant needs

When to harvest

Many seed packets include information to help gardeners care for their plants.

each vegetable was planted. This can help gardeners know when the plants are ready to be harvested.

Tending the Garden

Vegetables need water. Seeds should be watered twice a day. Once the plant is **established**, it can be watered a few times a week. Gardeners can touch the soil to decide if the plant should be watered. If the dirt is dry, the plant needs water.

Gardeners should water the bases of their plants. This allows the roots to absorb the water. It is best to water in the morning. This gives plants time to absorb the water before it gets hot.

Weeding is another important part of gardening. Weeds are plants that grow where they are not wanted. They steal water and nutrients from other plants. Weeds should be pulled up. Gardeners can grab them at their base. This helps get the roots out. Weeding is also a good time to check for pests.

Garden Helpers

Some bugs are good for gardens. Ladybugs, lacewings, and ground beetles eat garden pests. Gardeners should leave these insects alone. They protect gardens.

Some insects and snails eat vegetables. They can be squished or moved.

Harvesting

Harvesting is one of the most exciting parts of gardening! Different vegetables can be harvested at different times. Each plant has its own signs that it is ready to be harvested.

Leafy greens can be harvested once the leaves are big. A few leaves can be taken at a time. The rest of the plant will keep growing.

Tomatoes change colors as they ripen. To harvest, gardeners can gently twist them off the vine. Tomatoes should be harvested a little before they are ripe. This helps the plant make more tomatoes.

Gardeners should harvest vining plants, such as peas, very
gently to avoid damaging the rest of the plant.

Some people wait to harvest their carrots until the weather gets cold. This makes them taste sweeter.

Carrots are ready to be harvested 55 to 80 days after planting. When people are ready to harvest their carrots, they can break up the dirt around the carrots with a shovel. This helps loosen the soil. Then they can pull the carrots up by their leaves.

Vegetable gardening is a fun activity. It helps people learn about plants. It also gives gardeners a delicious reward.

Further Evidence

Watch the video at the website below. Does it give any new evidence to support Chapter Three?

Garden Health and Maintenance

abdocorelibrary.com/vegetable-gardens

Garden Plants

Tomato

Tomatoes are fruit vegetables. They can be eaten raw or made into sauces or soups.

Cucumber

Cucumbers are fruit vegetables. They can be eaten raw or made into soups or noodles.

Broccoli

Broccoli is an aboveground vegetable. It can be cooked or eaten raw.

Swiss chard

Swiss chard is an aboveground vegetable. Young leaves can be eaten in salads. Mature leaves can be chopped and put in soups.

Glossary

bulbs
rounded, layered parts of plants, such as onions, that grow underground and hold the plants' nutrients

climate
the long-term weather pattern of a certain area

edible
able to be eaten

established
having a well-developed root system

gradually
slowly

nutrients
substances that living things need to grow and stay healthy

tubers
starchy parts of plants, such as potatoes, that grow underground and hold the plants' nutrients

Online Resources

To learn more about growing vegetable gardens, visit our free resource websites below.

Visit **abdocorelibrary.com** or scan this QR code for free Common Core resources for teachers and students, including vetted activities, multimedia, and booklinks, for deeper subject comprehension.

Visit **abdobooklinks.com** or scan this QR code for free additional online weblinks for further learning. These links are routinely monitored and updated to provide the most current information available.

Learn More

Hämeenaho-Fox, Satu. *My First Garden*. DK, 2023.

Lim, Angela. *Fruit Gardens*. Abdo, 2026.

Philip, Claire. *Little Green Fingers*. Gestalten, 2023.

Index

About the Author

Matt Lilley has an MS in scientific and technical writing. The focus of his degree was on medical writing for kids. He loves researching and writing about all sorts of topics. He lives in Minnesota with his family.